Why Projects Fail

Uladzislau Shauchenka

Author

Uladzislau Shauchenka, project manager, PMP

Proofreading and editing

Camille Willock

Cory L. Kleinschmidt

Design and Layout

Almagreta (*www.almagreta.com*)

Contact

Official website: *www.whyprojectsfailbook.com*

Email: *uladzislau@gmail.com*

Table of contents

Introduction

Why Projects Fail is intended not only for those in project management or in business, but for everyone who wants to know why some projects fail while others succeed. It attempts to find the root causes which influence the outcome of every project.

This book was written to help you learn from the failure of others and avoid pitfalls yourself. It contains statistics, analyses, case studies, lessons learned and many facts and arguments.

The inevitability of project failure is a myth spread by unqualified and weak professionals. Projects can and should be successful, and there is no magic in doing project management the right way. The potential pitfalls can be learned and avoided with a simple set of guidelines.

1

Failure rate

Many projects fail, in fact, statistics show that projects fail more often than they succeed. And the reason they fail range from late delivery, over-budget, non delivery of product to some being totally cancelled before anything was produced.

> "Here is Edward Bear, coming downstairs now, bump, bump, bump, on the back of his head, behind Christopher Robin. It is, as far as he knows, the only way of coming downstairs, but sometimes he feels that there really is another way, if only he could stop bumping for a moment and think of it."
>
> — A.A. Milne

Statistics on failure rate are a good predictor of the success of projects.

The Robbins-Gioia Survey (2001) respondents included representatives from multiple industries such as government, information technology, communications, finance, utilities, and healthcare. The respondents viewed their Enterprise Resource Planning implementation as:

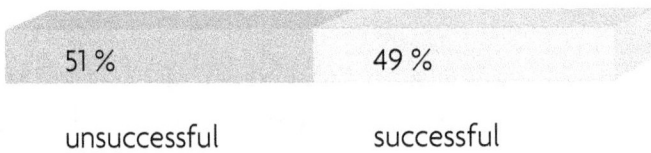

51 %	49 %
unsuccessful	successful

The Conference Board Survey (2001) interviewed executives at 117 companies that attempted ERP implementations:

failed to achieve their business case within one year of going live

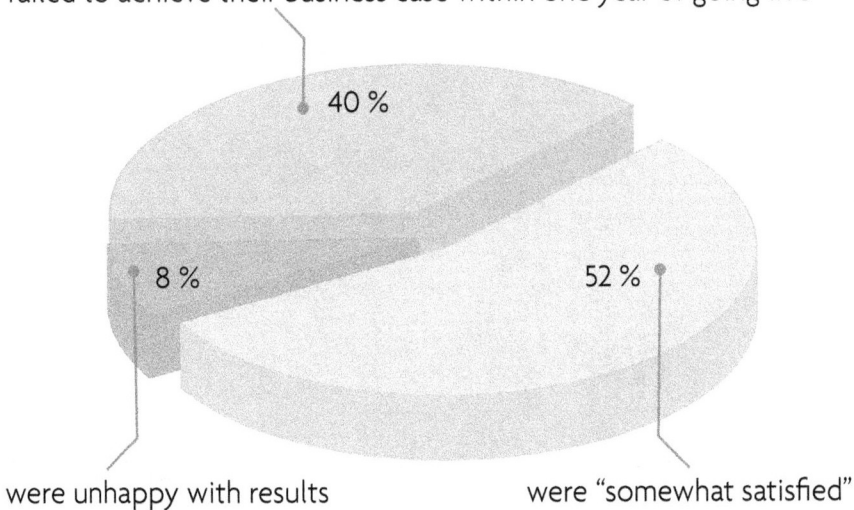

40 %

8 %

52 %

were unhappy with results

were "somewhat satisfied"

The KPMG Canada Survey (1997) respondents from Canada's leading 1,450 public and private sector organizations said about their projects that:

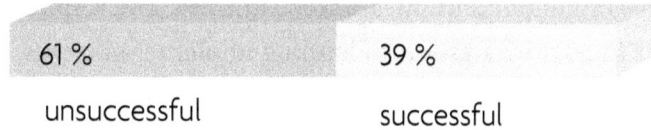

61 %	39 %
unsuccessful	successful

IT executives from banking, securities, manufacturing, retail and wholesale, health care, insurance, services, local, state and federal organizations who participated in the Standish Group's Chaos Report (1995) concluded:

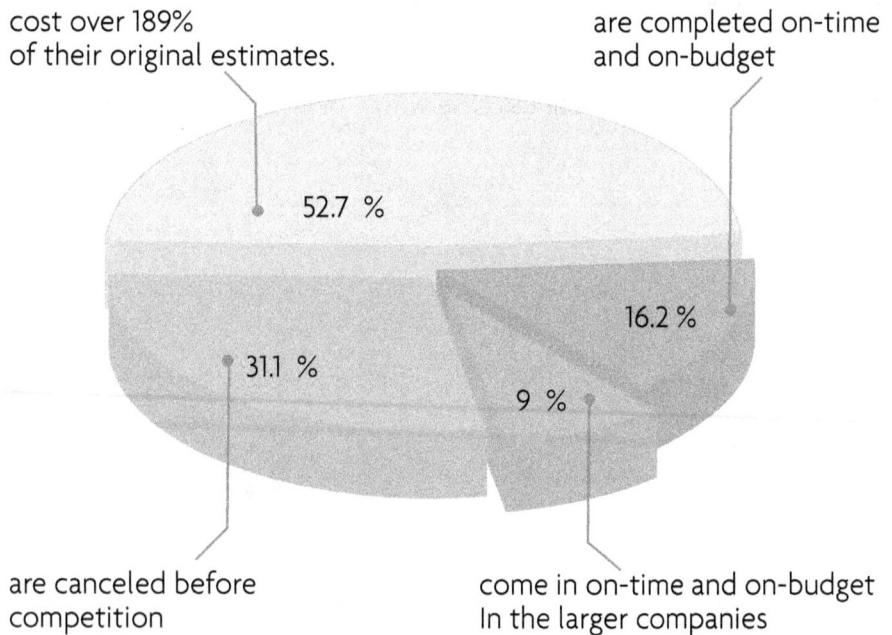

cost over 189% of their original estimates.

are completed on-time and on-budget

52.7 %

16.2 %

31.1 %

9 %

are canceled before competition

come in on-time and on-budget In the larger companies

2

List of failed projects

This is the non-exhaustive list of notable project failures. As you go through it you'll observe that project failure happens in every industry and in every geographical location. Both private and public companies suffer as a result of failed projects. Companies and agencies sometimes do everything to hide failed projects; and since lessons aren't learned, new projects suffer the same fate.

Year	Company	Cost	Outcome
2010	Lumber Liquidators	$14 million	Insufficient training of personnel on new SAP implementation resulted in lost sales.
2010	Virgin Airlines (Australia)	$20 million	Cloud hosting failure disrupted travel for 50,000 customers.
2010	EDS	$460.3 million	Fine paid to settle lawsuit over a failed CRM project for British Sky Broadcasting.
2008	J.Crew	$3 million	Severe problems following a website and call center upgrade caused revenue loss.
2007	Deloitte	$40 million	Poor requirements gathering and testing of LAUSD payroll system caused overruns.
2005	Hudson Bay Co. [Canada]	$33.3 million	Problems with inventory system led to loss.
2005	UK Inland Revenue	$3.45 billion	Software errors contributed to tax-credit overpayment.
2004	Avis Europe PLC [UK]	$54.5 million	Enterprise resource planning (ERP) system cancelled.
2004	Ford Motor Co.	$400 million	Purchasing system abandoned after deployment.
2004	J Sainsbury PLC [UK]	$527 million	Supply-chain management system abandoned after deployment.
2004	Hewlett-Packard Co.	$160 million	Problems with ERP system contributed to loss.
2003	AT&T Wireless	$100 million	Customer relations management (CRM) upgrade problems lead to revenue loss.
2002	McDonald's Corp.	$170 million	The Innovate information-purchasing system cancelled.

Year	Company	Cost	Outcome
2002	Sydney Water Corp. [Australia]	$33.2 million	Billing system cancelled.
2002	CIGNA Corp.	$445 million	Problems with CRM system contributed to loss.
2001	Nike Inc.	$100 million	Problems with supply-chain management system contributed to loss.
2001	Kmart Corp.	$130 million	Supply-chain management system cancelled.
2000	Washington. O.C.	$25 million	City payroll system abandoned after deployment.
1999	United Way	$12 million	Administrative processing system cancelled.
1999	State of Mississippi	$185 million	Tax system cancelled.
1999	Hershey Foods Corp.	$151 million	Problems with ERP system contributed to loss.
1998	Snap-on Inc.	$50 million	Problems with order-entry system contributed to revenue loss.
1997	U.S. Internal Revenue Service	$4 billion	Tax modernization effort cancelled.
1997	State of Washington	$40 million	Department of Motor Vehicle (DMV) system cancelled.
1997	Oxford Health Plans Inc.	$3.4 billion	Problems with billing and claims system led to loss in corporate value.
1996	Arianespace [France]	$350 million	Software specification and design errors caused Ariane 5 rocket to explode.

Year	Company	Cost	Outcome
1996	FoxMeyer Drug Co.	$40 million	ERP system abandoned after deployment, forcing company into bankruptcy.
1995	Toronto Stock Exchange [Canada]	$25.5 million	Electronic trading system cancelled.
1994	U.S. Federal Aviation Administration	$2.6 billion	Advanced Automation System cancelled.
1994	State of California	$44 million	DMV system cancelled.
1994	Chemical Bank	$15 million	Software error caused funds to be deducted from 100, 000 customer accounts.
1993	London Stock Exchange [UK]	$600 million	Taurus stock settlement system cancelled after 10 years of development.
1993	Allstate Insurance Co.	$130 million	Office automation system abandoned after deployment.
1993	London Ambulance Service [UK]	$25 million	First attempt to build dispatch system cancelled; second abandoned after deployment.
1993	Greyhound Lines Inc.	$61 million	Bus reservation system crashed repeatedly, contributing to revenue loss.
1992	Hilton Hotels. Marriott Int.	$165 million	Travel reservation system cancelled.
1994	Eurotunnel	$11.4 billion	The project of Channel Tunnel came in over its predicted budget.
1991	Canadian Passport Office	$17 million	Automation of Canadian Travel documents went twice over budget.

3

Main Elements of Project Failure

What are the criteria that define failed or successful projects? What are the main elements of project failure? Let's have a look at surveys and stats and then have a closer look at all of these project failure criteria.

According to The Bull Survey, conducted by the French computer manufacturer and systems integrator, among 203 project managers from the finance, IT, utilities, manufacturing, business services, and telecommunication services sectors in UK, the main project failure criteria are:

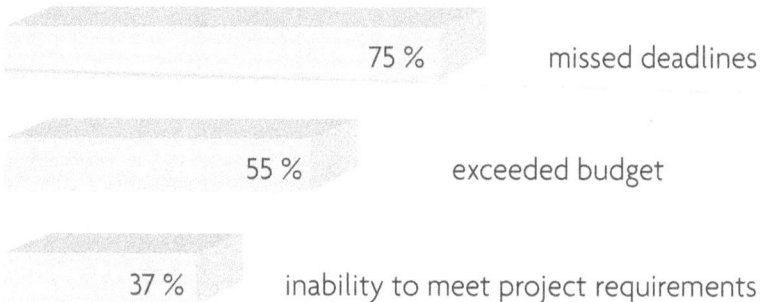

75 %	missed deadlines
55 %	exceeded budget
37 %	inability to meet project requirements

According to a Dynamic Markets survey of 800 IT managers, 62 percent of IT projects fail to meet their schedules. Reasons given are:

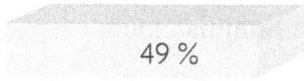

49 %   suffered budget overruns

47 %   had higher-than-expected maintenance costs

41 %   failed to deliver the expected business value

Cost overruns

Cost overrun is defined as excess of actual cost over budget. Cost overrun is common in infrastructure, building, and technology projects. One of the most comprehensive studies of cost overrun, by Bent Flyvbjerg, Mette Skamris Holm, and Søren Buhlthat, found:

- 9 out of 10 projects had overrun
- overruns of 50 to 100 percent were common
- overrun was found in each of 20 nations and five continents covered by the study
- overrun had been constant for the 70 years for which data were available

An industry study by the Standish Group (2004) found that the average cost overrun for IT projects was 43 percent, that 71 percent of projects were over budget, over time, and under scope; and that total waste was an estimated US$55 billion per year in the United States alone.

Cost overrun is typically calculated in one of two ways. Either as a percentage, namely actual cost minus budgeted cost, or as a ratio vis-a-vis actual cost divided by budgeted cost. For example, if the budget for building a new bridge was $100 million and the actual cost was $150 million, then the cost overrun may be expressed as 50 percent or by the ratio 1.5.

Spectacular examples of cost overrun:

The Sydney Opera House at 1,400 percent.

The Concorde supersonic airplane at 1,100 percent.

The cost overrun of Boston's Big Dig was 275 percent, or US$11 billion.

The cost overrun for the Channel tunnel between UK and France was 80 percent for construction costs and 140 percent for financing costs.

Cost overrun can be explained in three categories: technical, psychological, and political-economic. Technical explanations account for cost overrun in terms of imperfect forecasting techniques, inadequate data, etc.

Psychological explanations account for overrun in terms of an optimistic bias among forecasters.

Finally, political-economic explanations see overrun as the result of strategic misrepresentation of scope and/or budgets.

Business objective is not met

> "I would say that what we've gotten for a half billion dollars is an unpronounceable acronym [DIMHRS]".
>
> — U.S. Defense Secretary Robert Gates

The project objective consists of the business benefits that an organization expects to achieve as a result of spending time and exerting effort to complete a project. Project objectives are basically the reasons for doing the project and should not be confused with project products, i.e. deliverables. Generally, the project is considered successful if the project objectives are met successfully.

The reasons for not meeting a business objective are:

‣ The business objective is not aligned to one or more deliverables

‣ The project deliverables are not helping to satisfy the objective, so the objective cannot be successfully achieved

‣ Scope creep leading to deliverables not being aligned with the business objective

Uncontrolled changes in a project's scope occur when the scope is not properly defined, documented, or controlled.

Missed deadline

A target date is the result of a detailed project plan that clarifies the work to be done. The critical path through a network of tasks determines the earliest possible project completion date, assuming unlimited resources are available. The actual target date may be later, depending upon the project's priority and the availability of people and other resources.

> "How does a project get to be a year behind schedule? One day at a time."
>
> — Fred Brooks

Deadlines are missed for the same reason projects go over budget. Missed deadlines are directly related to cost overruns; when a project is delayed, costs are almost certain to increase. And while people might not understand whether a project achieves objectives or not, everyone understands deadlines and budgets.

The deadline should not be confused with the target date. When a deadline is missed, there is no longer any point in completing the commitment. Contest entry submission and Christmas eve advertising are pertinent examples of this. Thus, work on the project is stopped right away. On the other hand, when a target date is missed, the job should still be finished.

When management sets unrealistic deadlines right from the start, they are often missed no matter how hard the project team works.

Scope creep plays a great role both in cost overruns and missed deadlines. For example, when new features are added to already approved product designs without corresponding revisions to the schedule, budget or other resources.

4

Reasons
for project failure

It is obvious that projects fail for many reasons. Everyone working on a project has his own opinion about the ultimate causes of its failure. It is impossible to have two completely identical failed projects with the same scope, objective and unexpected situations. Knowing the causes of one project failure provides an opportunity to avoid pitfalls in future projects.

Should you be concerned about all of the potential reasons for project failure?

According to Pareto's principle, 20 percent of the defects are causing 80 percent of the problems. So if you learn what usually goes wrong on most of the projects, you can plan how to deal with it in advance. Knowledge of what can go wrong is your secret to the project's success.

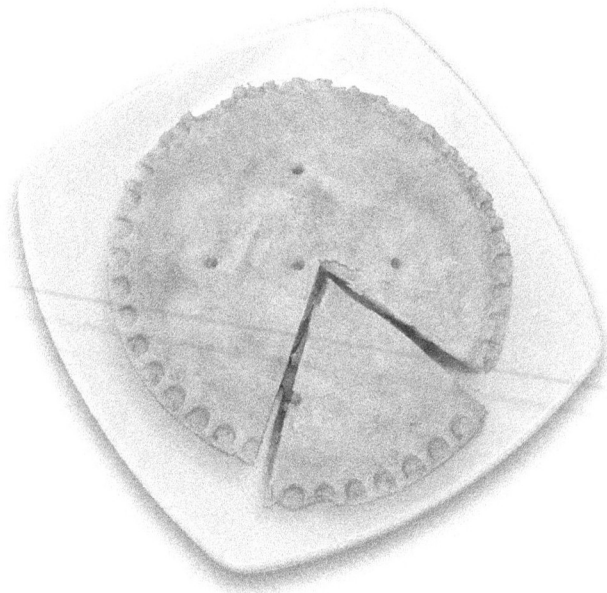

Pareto's principle

In 1906, Italian economist Vilfredo Pareto created a mathematical formula to describe the unequal distribution of wealth in his country, observing that twenty percent of the people owned eighty percent of the wealth. The principle that 20 percent of something is always responsible for 80 percent of the results, became known as Pareto's principle or the 80/20 Rule. The Pareto principle in project management reminds you to focus on the 20 percent that matters.

So what do the statistics say about the main reason for project failures?

According to the Coverdale Organization research (Cushing, 2002) the primary causes for project failure are:

▸ poor planning, including time or resource estimates
▸ unclear goals and objectives that change during the project
▸ lack of executive support and user involvement

The Bull Survey (1998) named the major causes of project failure as:

▸ breakdown in communication
▸ lack of planning
▸ inadequate coordination of resources
▸ poor quality control

The key findings of the KPMG Canada Survey (1997) regarding the reasons for project failure were:

▸ poor project planning
▸ weak business case
▸ lack of top management involvement and support

The Chaos Report (1995) lists as the top 3 reasons for project failure:

▸ incomplete requirements
▸ lack of user involvement
▸ lack of resources

In the OASIG Study (1995), the main reasons why systems fail to meet their objectives were identified as:

▸ lack of attention to the human and organizational aspects of it
▸ poor project management
▸ poor articulation of user requirements

5

Communication
Management

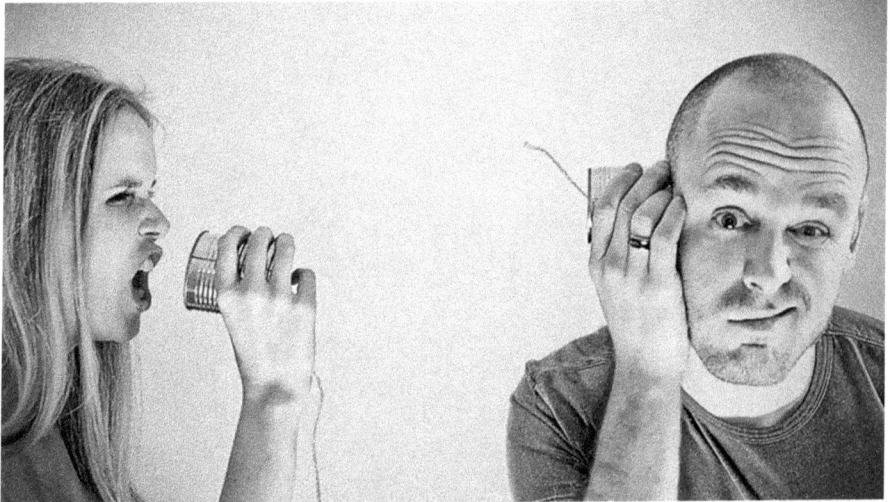

Project Communication Management plays a key role in keeping all members of the project management team on the same page. Improper project communication among all team members and project stakeholders will have a negative impact on the project outcome.

> "If I had to name a single all-purpose instrument of leadership, it would be communication".
>
> — John W Gardner

Communication is essentially the effective exchange of information from one project team member to another. Efficient communication should start from the moment a project is assigned and continue on a daily basis. Effective communication means that every project team member should be fully informed of the project status at all times.

The communication management plan details the communication needs and expectations for the project. It includes specific communication technologies to be used, such as an internal messaging system, weekly e-mail updates, conference calling, etc. The communication management plan also assigns team members responsibility for each format of communication.

When questioned about lessons learned after a project is completed, project teams often list communication as one of the most needed areas for improvement. On many occasions during troubled projects, project team members feel that if the communication had been better, the project would have run smoother.

Communication not only keeps everyone up-to-date on the progress of the project, but also facilitates buy-in and ownership of major project decisions and milestones. To ensure the success of a project, information such as expectations, risks, resources, status reports, and major change requests, needs to be communicated on a regular basis to all of the major stakeholders.

The project plan needs to determine what information should be communicated to all stakeholders in the project. That information must be available to the stakeholders in a proper form and without delays. Communication with project stakeholders must be managed so that all requirements are met and issues are promptly resolved.

It should also be taken into account that projects often do not have naturally formed teams, with team members sometimes even residing in different geographic locations. It is important to quickly implement effective communications among all affected parties by utilizing unique delivery methods and communication devices, no matter how complicated or diverse the project team may be.

Making assumptions

Making assumptions is the surest way to project failure. Every stakeholder of the project is important. Even minor stakeholders have the potential to negatively impact the project. It is often mistakenly assumed that everything is understood completely by everyone in the same way.

Unfortunately, people we communicate with tend to understand the message in their own way and act accordingly. Making assumptions that stakeholders or team members will understand ambiguous language as it is intended to be understood leads to unintentional misunderstanding and the need to rework to rectify it.

Often, a manager asks an employee to perform a certain task and believes that his instruction has been clearly understood. However, when the manager gets the results of the work, he finds it is not what he wanted. Typically the employee is blamed for the failure. In fact, the manager made assumptions and failed to ensure that his message was clearly understood.

When the information gets passed from individual to individual it gets distorted in the same way as in the children's game of Chinese whispers, where an initial message turns into a completely different message on its way from person to person.

It is crucial for project team members to develop active listening skills and not simply broadcast the information. They need to make sure the message is understood correctly and interpreted as intended by asking questions and confirming the message.

Not uncovering a hidden agenda

A hidden agenda is a secret plan serving an individual's own interests, regardless of how negatively it might affect others. Hidden agendas do not exist to serve the project; they exist to serve narrow and selfish interests. A hidden agenda may dictate decisions and actions.

It is a scary thought, but a stakeholder might go as far as to secretly work towards the failure of a project to serve his own interests. Or a stakeholder can underhandedly deal with a specific vendor regardless of whether or not prices from other vendors are lower.

Hidden agendas are common among stakeholders, and they can hinder the progress of a project and lower team morale. Project team members often get frustrated by unjustified decisions made by stakeholders with hidden agendas.

Stakeholders occupying executive positions in multiple companies are more likely to have hidden agendas. Projects more likely to suffer from hidden agendas are public projects because of their amount of government politics and absence of transparency and control. Projects with many stakeholders are at high risk of having hidden agendas too.

A clear sign of a hidden agenda on a project would be if a stakeholder opposing or supporting the project's functionality cannot clearly and objectively justify his decision. Delaying a decision on a key issue that requires a decision or feedback is another sign of hidden agenda.

These issues are difficult to address because people with hidden agendas are usually key stakeholders from upper management. The best thing to do is to consider hidden agendas as risks and plan accordingly.

6

Mars
Climate Orbiter

$ 125 million, crash on Mars.

? Poor communication, lack of testing.

The Mars Climate Orbiter was intended to enter orbit at an altitude of 140-150 km above Mars. However, a navigation error caused the spacecraft to reach as low as 57 km. Contact was lost and never re-established, and no further signal was ever received from the spacecraft.

Findings of the failure by the review board indicate that the navigation error was caused by the reporting of spacecraft data in imperial instead of metric units. This caused the spacecraft to miss its intended 140–150 km altitude above Mars during orbit insertion, and instead to enter the Martian atmosphere at about 57 km. At this low altitude, the spacecraft was destroyed by atmospheric stresses and friction.

The metric/imperial mix-up that destroyed the craft was caused by a human error in the software development, back on Earth. The thrusters on the spacecraft, which were intended to control its rate of rotation, were controlled by a computer that underestimated the effect of the thrusters by a factor of 4.45.

This is the ratio between a pound force (the standard unit of force in the imperial system) and a newton (the standard unit in the metric system). The software was working in pounds force, while the spacecraft expected figures in newtons (1 pound force equals approximately 4.45 newtons).

The software had been adapted from use on the earlier Mars Climate Orbiter, and was not adequately tested before launch. The navigation data provided by this software was also not cross-checked while in flight.

The Mars climate orbiter failure board released a report quoting the contributing causes of the failure of this project. These included inadequate consideration of the entire mission and its post-launch operation as a total system, inconsistent communications and training within the project, and lack of complete end-to-end verification of navigation software and related computer models.

In particular the board cited:

▸ the operational navigation team was not fully informed on the details of the way that Mars Climate Orbiter was pointed in space, as compared to the earlier Mars Global Surveyor mission
▸ some communication channels among project engineering groups were too informal
▸ the small mission navigation team was oversubscribed and its work did not receive peer review by independent experts
▸ personnel were not trained sufficiently in certain areas, such as the relationship between the operation of the mission and its detailed navigational characteristics, or the process of filing formal anomaly reports
▸ the process to verify and validate certain engineering requirements and technical interfaces between some project groups, and between the project and its prime mission contractor, was inadequate.

7

Stakeholders Management

A stakeholder is anyone who has an interest in the project or will be affected by its deliverables. It is important to understand the values and issues that stakeholders have in order to address them and keep everyone on board for the duration of the project, ensuring that all of these various groups are supportive, committed and engaged.

Stakeholder management is about creating positive relationships with stakeholders through the appropriate management of their expectations and agreed objectives.

Stakeholder management is essential to a successful project. Projects can fail because the real stakeholders and key decision makers are uninvolved in determining project strategy and direction. The opinions of stakeholders should be used to shape a project at an early stage, keep support throughout the lifecycle of the project and improve its quality.

Stakeholder Management includes:

‣ Stakeholder Identification - Interested parties, either internal or external, to the organization/project
‣ Stakeholder Analysis - Recognizing stakeholders' needs, authority, and common relationships
‣ Stakeholder Matrix - Positioning stakeholders according to the level of influence and impact
‣ Stakeholder Engagement - Agreement on a common set of values and principles

Stakeholder engagement is very effective if it is done in person during a presentation, but this is not always possible. Online and phone communication should be used to engage stakeholders on a regular cycle such as every week or month, or based on key project events or milestones.

In January 1996 the Gartner Group, in their paper Project Management Skills: Avoiding Management by Crisis, identified insufficient involvement of stakeholders and infrequent communication with sponsors as leading causes of project failure.

Quite often, project managers have to work on a project without having the necessary authority. The authority to effectively influence others is crucial for project success. Building consensus, managing stakeholder expectations, and translating a concept into a range of options for achieving project goals is impossible without the necessary level of Project Management authority.

Understanding stakeholders' needs, levels of influence, and perceptions requires strong communication and people skills. All of the stakeholders have their own agenda when it comes to the project deliverables. Some see the project as an opportunity and want the project to succeed, while others see it as a threat and prefer to see the project fail.

> All projects need agreement on: who decides the requirements, who provides the budget, who provides the resources, who authorizes any changes, and who defines the required standards.

The project sponsor works with the project manager to identify all key stakeholders. Large projects can have a project board which consists of key stakeholders to support the project sponsor. Stakeholders come from many areas of the business: senior management, human resources, finance, and marketing. A stakeholders' interest in the project is focused on his or her area.

Not clearly defined deliverables

The critical success factor for any project is to define clear deliverables. This is obvious: if you don't know what you are supposed to do, how can a project ever succeed? It's one of the reasons so many projects fail: the requirements aren't defined or clearly documented.

> "If you don't know how to do a task, start it, then ten people who know less than you will tell you how to do it."
>
> — Unknown

Project managers should collaborate with key stakeholders to define specific detailed project requirements and deliverables. Defining specific project requirements is necessary to align project goals to business goals. The project should have clear and specific project objectives as well. Although stakeholders are not always eager to participate, at this stage engaging them will help ensure success.

While defining project deliverables and setting project objectives may seem obvious, many companies skip this stage in order to jumpstart a project. Business executives assume the requirements are met without performing any confirming analysis. These projects are likely to fail and the companies usually encounter over-spending, rework, and unmet expectations.

Any project needs a clear set of deliverables to achieve the project goals and objectives. These should be communicated clearly to the stakeholders. It is important to ensure that a clear understanding of the quality and composition of each deliverable exists. Prototypes and samples can help deter misunderstanding or disappointment later.

A clear description of all intermediate and final project deliverables is crucial. Project deliverables include all product deliverables plus project specific items, such as progress reports, completed checklists, glossaries, etc. Key stakeholders must review the definition of deliverables and must agree they accurately reflect what must be delivered.

Saying yes to every request

Stakeholders often change their minds about what must be delivered. Sometimes the business environment changes after the project starts, so assumptions made at the beginning of the project may no longer be valid. This often means the scope or deliverables of the project need to change. If all changes are accepted, however, the project would inevitably go over budget and behind schedule, and might never be completed.

Weighted decisions should be made on whether or not to incorporate the changes immediately or in the future, or to reject them. Controlling how the changes are incorporated and allocating resources accordingly increases the chances of project success. Failing to manage changes effectively is a common reason why projects fail.

> "You can't just ask customers what they want and then try to give that to them. By the time you get it built, they'll want something new."
>
> — Steve Jobs

The later a project change is made, the more difficult it will be to implement without significant repercussions. The ramifications of the change will also vary proportionally to the size of the change. Minor adjustments may have a negligible effect, but a significant change in scope could set a long project back several weeks, months, or even years.

> "I can't give you a sure-fire formula for success, but I can give you a formula for failure: try to please everybody all the time".
>
> — Herbert Bayard Swope

Anything that alters the project's planned dates, budget, deliverables, or customer expectations must be documented and approved before implementation. Each change must be evaluated in terms of impact and approved by the Sponsor. Often, when they realize the impact that this change will have on the project, they decide not to proceed.

The change management process is key to the successful outcome of a project. The process ensures that each change introduced is properly defined, considered and approved before implementation. Although this procedure will not remove all risks, it will enable some changes to be made with minimal disruption. A change management procedure should include:

‣ identifying the need for change
‣ change recommendation
‣ analysis of the feasibility of change
‣ steering committee approval
‣ project sponsor approval
‣ implementing the change
‣ continue constant review

The final task is to communicate the revised change management plan to all project team members and stakeholders, explaining the rationale where resistance is encountered. It is also important at this point to ensure that the duration of meetings, decisions reached and agreements made are documented and retained.

Everyone on the project team should know and have respect for the boundaries of the project. The team should defend the project deliverables as specified in the contract or the project management plan. There should be a procedure in place for handling additional features and other requests for expanding the project scope. The proposed changes could be rolled into another, subsequent project that is separately funded and has its own schedule.

Lack of sponsor involvement and expertise

> "Tell me and I'll forget; show me and I may remember; involve me and I'll understand."
>
> — Chinese Proverb

Lack of an effective project sponsor guarantees project failure. High-level project sponsorship is necessary to support many aspects of the project, including realistic planning, change control, and the introduction of new practices. The sponsor is the owner of the project's business case and the setter of the agenda for the project. The sponsor should ensure that any obstacles faced by a project are dealt with.

> The project sponsor needs to be competent in preparation of the business case, investment and project briefs, procurement strategies, development of specifications, rules and regulations, etc.

Lack of sponsor buy-in often leads to reduced priority and visibility among other initiatives, failed escalation paths, and a strong potential for cost overruns. The Project Sponsor should understand the full scope of the project, both from a technical and business perspective. The Sponsor must know about the potential obstacles, risks, and issues on an on-going basis and should be able to act effectively.

Training project sponsors on their role in ensuring project success increases the likelihood of project excellence. This type of training provides sponsors with an understanding of what they should do to help manage project issues and to provide timely approvals. When project sponsors are on site, resources are more likely to be allocated in accordance with project importance.

The success of any project depends on the leadership and motivation given by project sponsors. A project sponsor is responsible for the day-to-day management of the client's interests in the project. The project sponsor's role as the interface between the business and the project team is critically important. When the interface between ownership and delivery is poorly managed, it is difficult to manage the project's critical success criteria – for example, to identify risks that could lead to time and cost overruns in time for corrective action to be taken.

8

Sewage Treatment System

$100 million, 3x budget.

? Unrealistic expectations, repeated redesigns, contracting problems.

Fallujah is 40 miles west of Baghdad and in the long-volatile Anbar province. The US Army destroyed the city, then committed to rebuilding it. The $100 million sewage-treatment system project in Fallujah, Iraq is three years late, triple its budgeted costs, and not even close to delivering on its goals.

Sewage continues to run in the streets, and the Special Inspector General for Iraq Reconstruction found that the system may never be properly connected to individual homes, lacks the necessary fuel to operate, and is unlikely to ever cover the full city.

What are the reasons for this project failure?

" Inspection quotes "unrealistic U.S. expectations from the start, repeated redesigns of the project, financial and contracting problems, and lack of good contractors to draw from".

Auditors found that in addition to the security problems it faced, the project was derailed after it was twice redesigned, costs skyrocketed, and the U.S. government was paralyzed by "indecision" about what to do.

The investigation into what went wrong with the wastewater project reads like a catalog of failings: staggering waste, endless delays, U.S. and Iraqi incompetence in contracting and administering the job, suspected sectarian discrimination, and worse-than-poor contractor performance. Intense violence overlaid it all.

Once scheduled for completion in January 2006, the project, which had a budget of $32.5 million, was supposed to be finished in April 2010. Meanwhile, costs have shot up to $98 million.

It was originally intended to cover all 24,400 dwellings in Fallujah, but will serve only 9,300 houses, about 38% of the city, at a cost of more than $10,000 a home. But despite all the money allocated, no funds have been set aside to connect the homes to the sewer system.

The Iraqi government, which was supposed to pay for the individual connections, now wants homeowners to bear the cost. But the auditors' report found that homeowners might knock holes through manhole walls and rig their own connections to the sewer, damaging the entire system.

The new design Iraqis wanted — a mechanized system, as opposed to open lagoons — will be powered by generators that take 6,000 gallons of fuel a day. No money is committed now for buying the fuel.

The initial contractor, FluorAmec of Greenville, S.C., was removed from the project after a year. That company was replaced with a string of local contractors.

9

Proper
Project Management

> "If you have procedures that haven't changed in 30 days then the manager is stealing from the company because he is not doing his job".
>
> — Taichi Ohno

The company doesn't have proper project management if its projects are late, over budget, or not meeting agreed upon requirements. What are other signs of trouble regarding project management in the company? The project management is applied in a reactive manner and is not seen as providing value. The projects are eventually completed, but with heavy stress and overtime work.

A proper project management process sets up an established system for communication between team members, project managers and clients.

The very nature of a project assumes an agreed-upon course of action to obtain the desired result.

Ensuring that a project stays on track requires constant communication with the various team members responsible for each part of the project. Having a clearly identified project leader, means clients have a direct and known point of contact with whom to communicate.

Most often, the project goes over time or over budget as a result of scope creep. Scope creep happens when a project continually evolves beyond the initial scope of work. The uncontrollable growth of a project scope is the result of a lack of project management, and it guarantees the failure of a project. In a successful project, flow of the project is controlled and team members are kept focused on the original scope of work as the project develops.

Potential risks or threats to the success of the project are identified early through the proper project management process. Understanding the possible areas that can sabotage a project helps to make decisions from the start and contributes to a completion that is on time and within budget.

If a problem threatens to derail the project when it is underway, project managers and team members must have a clearly defined plan to make timely decisions and resolve the problem or mitigate the potential risks.

"Of all the things I've done, the most vital is coordinating the talents of those who work for us and pointing them towards a certain goal".

— Walt Disney

Most projects require coordination of resources and if it is not carefully planned, things will be done in the wrong order or there will be constant conflict. All of that in the end will consume a lot more resources than necessary.

The real value of proper project management is in the quality of the end results and the avoidance of unnecessary delays and extra costs which means stakeholder and customer satisfaction.

Project Management
is more than conventional wisdom

When the company says they don't need a project manager, they probably don't understand the consequences of this decision. A project manager is a necessity, not an overhead. In fact the first person appointed on a project should be the project manager. If the project starts without a project manager, much of what has been done could be wasted time and effort.

A project is a temporary endeavor, having a defined beginning and end, undertaken to meet unique goals and objectives, to bring beneficial change or added value. The temporary nature of projects stands in contrast with business operations, which are repetitive, permanent functional work to produce products or services. In practice, the management of these two systems is quite different, and as such requires the development of distinct technical skills and the adoption of separate management.

The skills of a project manager are different in comparison to operational management skills. An operational manager does not necessarily make a good project manager - and vice versa. Project management is about focusing everyone on a goal, and managing the resources and workload to achieve that goal in a deadline driven environment. Projects require trained professionals with project management expertise.

> "The secret is to work less as individuals and more as a team. As a coach, I play not my eleven best, but my best eleven."
>
> — Knute Rockne

A project manager is responsible for all aspects of the planning, development and management of a project, from the initiating of the project to the day-to-day planning and management. The project manager has the authority to control all aspects of the project, including cost, risks and contractors.

Often scientists, engineers, and salespeople act in the role of project manager. While they are very good at what they do and have the technical knowledge, they cannot properly manage a project without training and practice. An accidental project manager is a person who is placed into the role by organizational necessity and chance, rather than by design or through choice of career path.

Managing people in a day-to-day business environment is usually much easier than on a project. If an employee has the same work they know how to do, the management effort is not significant. However, if an employee is not trained for the job, it is not their main job, or they have other priorities, management is more difficult.

On top of this, when there is any uncertainty, there is stress. On a project there are usually different functional representatives with different priorities and different expectations. If you add to this workload fluctuation, you'll get a major management issue.

Considering PM
as added time and cost

So what is the value that project management offers? Does project management add cost or cut it? For many people, the structured process of project management represents unwelcome change that is both demanding and costly.

In reality, successful project management ensures that goals are effectively accomplished for the benefit of the company. The project manager is there to guarantee the success of the project and to identify a potential point of failure and correct it, so that the project remains on track.

A project manager on a project becomes a designated point of contact for questions and concerns. The project manager is also able to monitor the critical actions and responsibilities of other team members.

The value of proper project management includes:

▸ better expectation-setting through more accurate estimating, planning and project definition

▸ faster execution through the reuse of common processes and templates

▸ fewer project problems encountered when utilizing proactive project management processes

▸ better organizational decision making through more effective project communication

▸ higher client satisfaction and less rework by building a higher quality product the first time

Structured accountability helps to ensure that the project stays on track and on schedule.

A key benefit of the successfully managed project, is that it is delivered within budget. From the scope of work and an estimated approved budget to the completion, costs for the project can inflate tremendously without proper project management processes. Effective project management provides measures not only to save money on a project, but to ensure resources are available for other projects.

"Be a yardstick of quality. Some people aren't used to an environment where excellence is expected."

— Steve Jobs

Projects that drag beyond a projected completion date can negatively impact everything from revenues to cash reserves. The value of project management is that it provides a way for setting specific goals within realistic timeframes.

Hiring PM after projects became a mess

"I'm a project manager, not a magician. Magicians have way cooler hats."

— Merlin Mann

A project manager should be hired as soon as the decision is made to start the project. Project management is not only about project execution and control. The most important part of successful projects is the analysis and planning. If the project manager skips this stage, it could be too late to catch up.

That is why it is already too late to hire a project manager when a project starts without one. What is the best solution when the project starts without a project manager? Cancel the project and start from scratch with proper processes, tools and techniques.

Most of the time a project manager is a project owner who is responsible for the leadership of the project from inception to completion. The project manager leads the team and helps negotiate the multiple relationships within any project and functions as the hub of a project.

A project manager must have a vision for the goals of the project. This should apply not only to the process, but also to the strategy. Because the project manager keeps an eye on the big picture from day one, he should be able to effectively lead the project's strategy as well.

Hiring a project manager before the project starts will not solve all management issues of the company, but it will enable smoother processes and better workflow. Finding the right team, giving appropriate direction, and managing the working environment while maintaining a strategic focus and staying on top of deadlines and deliverables are all part of a project manager's role.

> "The remarkable position in which we find ourselves is that we don't actually know what we actually know."
>
> — Bill Bryson

Using proper project management techniques and processes will give the project a higher likelihood that it will be completed on time, within budget, and to an acceptable level of quality.

eHealth Ontario

$ 4.8 million, no deliverables

? improper project management, poor contracting procedures.

eHealth Ontario was created to facilitate the development of a public Electronic Health Record system for all patients in the province by 2015. The agency was created in September 2008 out of a merger between the Ontario Ministry of Health's electronic health program and the Smart Systems for Health Agency (SSHA).

eHealth Ontario has been plagued by delays and its CEO was fired over a multimillion-dollar contracts scandal in 2009. Ontario CEO Sarah Kramer had approved about $4.8 million in no-bid contracts during the first four months of the agency's operation, while also spending $50,000 to refurnish her office and paying consultants up to $300 an hour.

Kramer billed thousands of dollars for limousine rides, including one $400 trip from Toronto to London, Ontario, before she resigned from her $380,000-a-year job in June. She was given a $317,000 severance package and received a $114,000 bonus after just 10 months on the job.

Nine senior eHealth employees were fired, reportedly for challenging the agency's tendering practices. eHealth Ontario argued that the no-bid contracts were necessary due to the rapid transition process to eHealth from its predecessor Smart Systems for Health Agency. The

opposition argued that the Ontario government spent five years and $647 million on the Smart Systems for Health Agency, which used 15 percent of its $225-million annual budget on consultants despite employing 166 people with annual salaries exceeding $100,000, before the project was shut down and restarted as eHealth Ontario.

Ontario Auditor General Jim McCarter reported on the eHealth Ontario spending scandal charges that successive governments wasted $1 billion in taxpayer money on underused computer systems and untendered contracts.

The report says that the board of directors at eHealth Ontario felt it had little power over CEO Sarah Kramer because she had been hired by Chair Alan Hudson "with the support of the Premier". That, McCarter said, gave Kramer the impression she had approval to ignore normal procurement procedures.

McCarter says the province was "lacking in strategic direction and relying too heavily on external consultations". At one point, the auditor writes, the eHealth program branch had "fewer than 30 full-time employees but was engaging more than 300 consultants".

Consultants were contracted by eHealth at up to $2,750 a day. They then billed taxpayers for out-of-pocket expenses that included $1.65 for a cup of tea and $3.99 for cookies. Some of the consulting costs incurred at eHealth include:

‣ $2,700-a-day consultant, charging $3.26 for a muffin and tea

‣ $300-an-hour consultant, charging for reading an article on electronic health records given to her by her husband, another consultant

‣ two consultants serving as vice-presidents and flown regularly from homes in Alberta

‣ $1,700-a-day executive assistant

‣ consultants charging to watch an eHealth episode on TVO's The Agenda and "debriefing" on the Toronto subway

McCarter said charges that favoritism was shown toward certain companies "without giving other firms a chance to compete were largely true". He cites one example of a firm that bid 500 per cent more than the next qualified bidder and was invited to bid again. The auditor estimated that two-thirds of the value of all eHealth Ontario contracts were sole-sourced.

❝ "When you have a lack of oversight, that's a lack of appropriate management. When you get a lack of oversight, you get broken rules. It goes together like a horse and carriage".

One of the biggest problems with the province's electronic health drive was that for years there was no set of specific goals and targets on how Ontario would computerize medical records.

There are four main recommendations in the auditor general's report:

▸ eHealth Ontario needs a comprehensive strategic plan

▸ there needs to be more government oversight while allowing management day to day operational autonomy by having specific targeted goals, timelines with estimated costs and periodic progress reports

▸ eHealth and the ministry should have full-time staff with the technical expertise to oversee the electronic health record project and consultants should have clear "project deliverables" and greater oversight of contractors billing

▸ the agency and the ministry should have appropriate review mechanisms to ensure procurement policies are followed

11

Risk Management

All projects involve risk. Even well-prepared plans must be flexible enough to meet and overcome unexpected challenges. Risk should be thoroughly analyzed and quantified before and during a project; effective response strategies should be in place to deliver projects that meet stakeholder demands.

Risk management requires top-level management support, acknowledgment that risk is reality, and a commitment to identify and manage them. What differentiates the successful project from the failed one? It's the use of risk management to anticipate potential negative conditions, problems, and realities. Ineffective projects are forced to react to problems, effective projects anticipate them.

At the start of all projects, the potential impact of risk on cost and schedule is almost unlimited. Therefore, the choice is to either dedicate proper and timely attention to understanding and managing risk, or suffer its consequences down the road.

Risk management must:

▸ identify risks and risk owners
▸ evaluate the risk's probability and consequences
▸ prioritize the risk management efforts
▸ develop risk management plans
▸ track the risk management efforts and manage accordingly

Costly surprises can be avoided by focusing on potential risks in the planning stages of a project and implementing strategies that reduce the impact and probability of those risks happening. A proper risk management process makes it easier to keep the project on schedule and budget. It also helps to ensure that unavoidable risks are adequately treated.

Since all projects involve some degree of risk, a project risk management plan is necessary to define and document those procedures that will be used to manage risk throughout the life of the project. Risk can be defined as any factor that may potentially interfere with the successful flow of a project. By recognizing potential problems and responding with proper actions, most of these problems can be avoided.

Risk management is simply a practice of systematically selecting cost effective approaches for minimizing the effect of threat realization to the organization. All risks can never be fully avoided or mitigated simply because of financial and practical limitations. Therefore, all organizations have to accept some level of residual risks.

According to The International Organization for Standardization, risk management should:

▸ be part of decision making

▸ explicitly address uncertainty

▸ be systematic and structured

▸ be based on the best available information

▸ take into account human factors

▸ be dynamic, iterative and responsive to change

A project risk management plan should also specify who is responsible for managing the different areas of risk, how risks will be tracked through the project life cycle, how contingency plans will be implemented, and how project reserves will be allocated in order to handle risks.

Project size has an effect on the project risk management plan. Large projects normally require more detailed risk planning than smaller projects due to the bigger number and complexity of potential risks. Quite often, this requires developing and analyzing alternative strategies and strategy evaluation criteria.

Risks Remain Uncovered

How can risk management be improved? By improving the identification of early risks and using the effective methods of presenting and using this data. Many risk databases contain poor quality, partially complete or limited data. Often this results in a limited understanding of project risk, and consequently, little attention and resources are allocated to the management of risk. Risk data cannot be used by stakeholders. As a result, flawed risk identification processes foster a false sense of security relating to the delivery of a project.

> "The major difference between a thing that might go wrong and a thing that cannot possibly go wrong is that when a thing that cannot possibly go wrong goes wrong it usually turns out to be impossible to get at or repair"
>
> — Douglas Adams

In many projects, risks are identified and analyzed in a random, ad hoc way. While everyone is worried about the highest impact risks, which are very unlikely to occur; moderate risks are often overlooked. When this happens, unexpected risks arise that are neither assessed nor planned for but rather, are dealt with as emergencies.

Uncovering project risks should not only focus on threats but also on positive risks, identifying opportunities which add speed, better quality and profitability to the project. Responses to risk opportunities are the opposite of responses to threats. They focus on seeking out risks and exploiting them.

It is essential that potential risks are identified, categorized and evaluated very early in the preparation and planning stage. It is much more effective to identify risks and then group them into categories, or start with a list of categories and then identify potential risks within each category, instead of looking at each risk independently and randomly. This way potential impacts and potential responses can be discussed and agreed on.

Risks structured in groups based on similar patterns can help eliminate duplicates and uncover symptoms of more fundamental risk. It's crucial that risks are communicated to the team and stakeholders and that risk owners are assigned. The risk owner has the responsibility to deal with specific risks for the project, decrease threats and enhance opportunities. Risk owners should also face consequences for failures.

Failed projects show that risks fatal to the project came out of the blue and nobody was aware of them. Even if someone on the project was aware of the risks, this person didn't inform anyone else. That is why risk communication should be properly addressed at team meetings and communicated to the sponsor.

No Risks Prioritization

The project team should identify all known risks during the planning stage. For each risk, they should also determine the probability that the risk event will occur and the potential impact on the project. High risk events should have specific plans to prevent them from occurring in the first place. Medium risks should be evaluated and proactively managed.

> "Everything that can be counted does not necessarily count; everything that counts cannot necessarily be counted."
>
> — Albert Einstein

The risks may include not having the right level of expertise, unfamiliarity with the technology, and problems integrating smoothly with existing products or equipment. Often the expertise of the team that would be required to deal with risks is not evaluated. As a result, the team may not be able to handle occurred risks effectively, even though the initial forecast was positive.

A risk index can be used to track and prioritize risks based on:

▸ criticality

▸ the time available for action

▸ their effects on safety and security

▸ the risk index should define and assign weights to risk factors to track changing priorities

This happens when the planning team is not the project team that manages the project or when key team members leave the project and are replaced by individuals with different skills, experience and capabilities.

Each potential risk should be carefully analyzed and project team members evaluated to determine if they are capable of managing risk successfully. If any gaps are identified, appropriate corrective action must be taken. The capability must be monitored during the project and managed if necessary to ensure the required level of capability is maintained.

Ideally, risk prioritization is handled this way: the risks with the greatest loss and the greatest probability of occurring are handled first, and risks with lower probability of occurrence and lower loss are handled in descending order. In practice, balancing between risks with a high probability of occurrence but lower loss versus a risk with high loss but lower probability of occurrence can often be mishandled.

Risks must be prioritized because no project has the resources to mitigate every risk. The risks which pose the greatest threat to a project should receive priority. Risks must be continuously prioritized because of changing circumstances or external forces that change the priorities of particular risks.

No Contingency Plans

The KPMG study found that 55 percent of failed projects did no risk management at all. Usually a brief risk assessment is done when a new project is proposed for approval. Any identified high risk factors are analyzed to determine whether actions can be taken to eliminate, reduce or constrain the risk before the project starts. This may require adjustments to the proposed project's scope, objectives, timelines or resources.

> ▶ mitigation strategies are proactive actions to reduce either the probability of a risk occurring or its impact
>
> ▶ contingency plans are the alternative plans that will be executed when mitigation strategies fail

Once a project is approved, a Risk Management Plan should be developed for all risk factors that were not eliminated during the project proposal process. A Risk Management Plan includes a description of the risk, the impact of the risk on the project, what actions can be taken to assist in reducing the risk and, if necessary, a contingency plan. The Project Sponsor and stakeholders must be involved in the proactive reduction of risk.

Risk avoidance, risk minimization and risk acceptance are the main options to deal with risk. Avoiding risks means to organize the project in such a way that it does not encounter a risk at all. This could mean changing a supplier or adopting a different technology or, if there is a fatal risk, terminating a project. Risk minimization can be achieved by eliminating the causes of risks or decreasing the negative effects resulting from the occurred risks. Risk acceptance is a final choice if the risk effects on the project are minimal or the possibilities to influence it prove to be very difficult, time consuming or too expensive.

If the risk is caused by poor system scope, whole sections of the risk list will be dropped by eliminating non-essential requirements. Technology can be acquired to reduce the risk of building particular functionality. Finally, risk can be transferred to other organizations. Typically, the risk itself comes from lack of information and therefore the mitigation strategy consists of investigating the topic further to reduce the uncertainty.

Contingency plans include specific strategies and actions to deal with a particular problem or emergency. They also include a monitoring process and "triggers" for initiating planned actions. A contingency plan is needed when risk avoidance and risk transfer have failed, mitigation was not successful, and the risk must be addressed head-on. This happens very often with indirect risks, i.e. risks over which the project has no control. It could also happen when the mitigation strategies are too costly to implement.

12

Canadian Gun Registry

1 billion, 500x budget.

Poor communication, risk management, and requirements analysis.

The Canadian Firearms Registry was intended to be a list of all gun owners in Canada and the firearms they possess. The project was started as an effort to reduce crime by making every gun traceable. Police officers can search an online database to see which guns a suspect owns, while the RCMP would use the information to trace the ownership of weapons used in crimes.

The incident that triggered the need for the gun registry was Marc Lepine's massacre of 14 women at Montreal's École Polytechnique in 1989. Pressure from students and families of the victims spurred politicians to pass Bill C-68 in 1995, which included the registry.

In December 2002, the Auditor General of Canada reported that the project was running vastly above initial cost estimates. The report shows that the implementation of the firearms registry program has had significant strategic and management problems.

The proper analysis was not conducted, and had it been a private company, it would have gone bankrupt. A planned relocation of the headquarters of the Canadian Firearms Centre from Ottawa to Edmonton had been scrapped because of rising program costs.

It was originally expected that the project needed only $2 million of investments while registration fees would cover the rest. In 1995, the Department of Justice reported to Parliament that the system would cost $119 million to implement, and that the income generated from licensing fees would be $117 million. This gave a net cost of $2 million.

At the time of the 2002 audit, the revised estimates from the Department of Justice revealed that the cost of the program would be more than $1 billion by 2004/05 and that the income from license fees in the same period would be $140 million. The annual operating costs of the program are reported to be $15 – $80 million.

This raises serious questions about how accurately the initial estimates had been calculated, or whether they hand been done at all. The cost overruns have been blamed on the inexperience of the Justice Department in managing a project of such scale. The main reason for cost overruns was that the scope of the project changed continuously.

Initially, the estimated cost of the Gun Registry project was just 2 million dollars. Obviously, the reason for the actual cost skyrocketing, was the unrealistically low estimate given in the first place.

Numerous reasons exist for the cost overrun including a failure to anticipate problems and poor risk management.

According to the Auditor General, The Canadian Gun Registry project had huge communication problems.

Canadian Gun Registry project cost breakdown by Canada's Fireart Center.

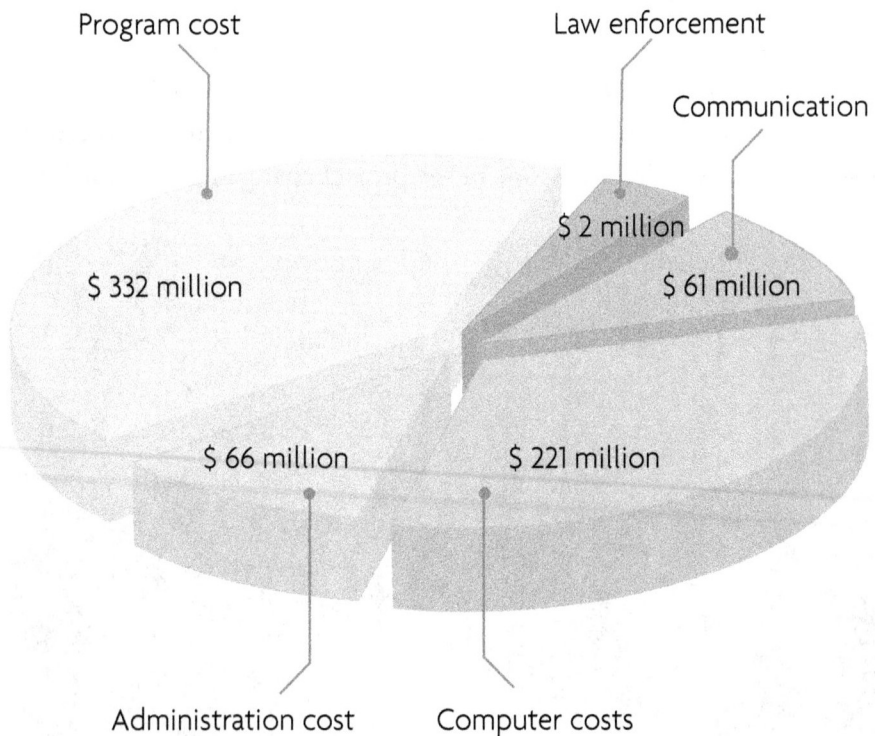

Program cost

Law enforcement

Communication

$ 2 million

$ 61 million

$ 332 million

$ 66 million

$ 221 million

Administration cost

Computer costs

Why Projects Fail Uladzislau Shauchenka *www.whyprojectsfailbook.com*

"The issue here is not gun control. And it's not even astronomical cost overruns, although those are serious. What's really inexcusable is that Parliament was in the dark. I question why the [Justice] department continued to watch the costs escalate without informing Parliament and without considering alternatives."

— Auditor General Sheila Fraser in her December 2002 report

13

Inadequate
Resources

One of the most important factors that defines the success or failure of a project is resources. Time, budget, available hardware, team member skills or vendor capability are all decisive factors in what direction the project will take. All these factors equate to money and the amount of money the company is prepared to spend does affect what resources are available to the project.

It's important for everyone involved in the project to understand the project's business case and purpose. What kind of business goals should be achieved and what financial return will justify the project? This analysis goes beyond discovering which of the standard project delivery goals is most important.

The team plays a crucial role as a recourse needed for successful project completion. Not having the right team members or having the team with the wrong skill mix can be a cause of project failure. The proper resources should be provided, either from internal staff or, if necessary, by hiring externally. Roles and responsibilities have to be clearly defined, more so when staff is hired externally.

Time is a big factor in the success or failure of a project. The surest path to a project failure is deciding on a non-negotiable deadline date prior to start of the project. This results in a rush to get started on the assumption that the sooner the project begins the sooner it will be finished. It is impossible to complete a project efficiently working backward from the project end date. Proper scheduling is absolutely necessary before the start of the project.

If the procurement process is not conducted properly it can jeopardize the project. Many projects have a "lowest price most successful candidate" policy, or an unrealistically low budget, not based on the true requirements. Only a supplier or team that has a proven track record of delivery within a budget is beneficial for the project. A structured due diligence should be conducted to ensure the right vendor selection. Transparency and open communication with all stakeholders are crucial elements to employ, in order to avoid the power influencer game in awarding the deal to a preferred vendor.

One of the best strategies for managing project problems is to recognize and address them early before they escalate. Successfully addressing a problem early may save you many more resources associated with having to deal with a chronic problem later.

Improper estimation or administration cuts

Underestimating of the time needed to complete a project will not only put it at risk to miss its deadline, but team members will also be put under stress. People usually accept occasional overtime work to complete a project. If this becomes routine, however, they will find ways to get out of work responsibilities during the workday. In turn it will require more over-scheduling. Team members have basic needs such as dentist appointments, grocery shopping and other domestic chores to complete. They must also make time for socializing and interacting with their families. All these factors are why proper allocation of time for the project is so important.

Cost estimation needs to be done well before the start of project development. Failure to budget for the cost of the project results in complete disaster. It is important to include all expenses for the project, such as the infrastructure cost, development tools cost, and hardware cost. For a software project, for example, cost estimation includes the cost of effort, the hardware and software cost, training the employees and customer, travelling to the customer, and networking and communication costs.

The use of an inappropriate cost estimation methodology would be another reason for project failure. No single methodology is better than another. Every methodology has its own strong and weak points which should be considered. The more methodologies are used to estimate the cost of a project, the more accurate estimates would be produced.

Initial estimates are rarely detailed and precise. The only time when the effort, cost, and duration of the project is known for sure is when the project is complete. Until then, every project has some measure of estimating uncertainty and risk. A contingency budget is used to compensate for the estimating uncertainty. For example, if the estimates are 80 percent accurate, a contingency budget should not be less than 20 percent.

Any project with deadlines or resource limits which have no bearing on reality, is doomed to failure. Often it is an imposed delivery deadline from the sponsor that is not realistic based on the prior estimates. The project manager has several options in this situation: renegotiate the deadline (project delay), employ additional resources (increased cost), or reduce the scope of the project (less delivered).

The project sponsor should be fully aware of the consequences of starting the project relying not on the estimates, but rather on artificially placed cuts and deadlines. Hardly any project survives improper estimation or administrative cuts without suffering in quality, customer satisfaction, cost overruns and stress put on the team.

Mistakes in contracting

Procurement is one of the most important stages of any project and has many potential pitfalls. During procurement the vendor is selected and technology is recommended by the vendor. If the company does not select the right vendor, there is a distinct chance that the project will be a failure. Sometimes project managers are not included in the procurement process, but they should always be key members of the procurement team, even if they rely on others with legal and purchasing expertise.

> "You need to understand what you are buying, and why, how it will affect your business, and what the potential risks are. That detailed understanding may be beyond the scope of a procurement department."
>
> — Owen Williams.

Procurement documents such as the requests for bids, requests for quotes, requests for proposals must accurately describe the work to be completed by the vendor, the evaluation techniques for the vendor and the methods to evaluate the contracted deliverables. Both the product scope and project scope should be addressed in the vendor's contract, as well as the roles and responsibilities of the members of the vendor's team.

Due diligence is one of the most important activities needed to be done during procurement to avoid project failure. Due diligence entails the thorough investigation of all aspects of the vendor in order to ensure the success of a contract.

It can include evaluation of capabilities, such as proof of concept and proof of technology, evaluation of team member skills ensuring that similar profiles will be carrying out the work, ability to start the project within a given time frame, credibility and references, and similar project experiences. Constraints, challenges, technology limitations, and vendor business sustainability should be evaluated as well to ensure that the vendor is strong enough to survive the project duration.

Some projects fail because of miscalculation and poor analysis of what part of the project should be contracted versus what part should be done internally. Selecting a wrong contract type, such as time and material contract instead of fixed price contract, can be a deadly mistake.

Some vendors use certain tricks to win projects, such as touting their products, experience, and skills. To avoid a situation when the vendor turns out to be incapable after the project starts, the project's cash flow can be based on milestones rather than time.

The evaluation criteria should be categorized into main areas such as cost, scope, timeline or strategy. The weight for each category should be assigned based on sponsor and key stakeholder inputs about what is important and what can be given less priority.

If the wrong evaluation criteria are developed, the vendors will be assessed against a wrong scale and the wrong vendor would have been selected. The more complex the evaluation criteria, the more likely there will be a problem selecting the right vendor.

The entire selection process can take a completely different direction if an influencer among key stakeholders plays his or her own game and awards the deal to a specific vendor. Any bias or subjective criteria puts the entire project at great risk. The only way to prevent that from happening is to enforce open and transparent communication policy with the sponsor and vendor evaluators.

It is important to monitor and control the procurement process. This includes proper review and evaluation of performance reports. Any changes to the contract should be evaluated and properly communicated before the final decision to proceed is made. The stage of verifying and accepting deliverables is also very important.

Team Capability

One of the most important steps of a project is to carefully choose the team. The team members should meet specific criteria and be able to perform at the level required for the project. It seems obvious but many projects fail simply because team members are chosen by sympathy or personal taste rather than objective criteria.

> "The way a team plays as a whole determines its success. You may have the greatest bunch of individual stars in the world, but if they don't play together, the club won't be worth a dime."
>
> — Babe Ruth

The single most important element of team composition is having a team that works together effectively. Collaboration and communication skills are two of the most critical personal skills demanded of all members. The ability and willingness to recognize and value the different roles and contributions of team members are essential.

Top two things people want in their work:

▸ public recognition as a contributing member of a worthy enterprise

▸ recognition and reward for their accomplishments

If the project team members have a lot of interaction with the client and therefore with scope-change requests, they must detect scope changes when they occur and follow the proper change management process. If they decide to take on the extra work themselves, there is a good chance that their activities will be completed late and jeopardize the entire project.

The specific, measurable and realistic goals for teams are absolutely essential to the success of the project. If goals are not set, then the first goal of the team is to develop goals and gain approval. Establishing the goals and making them known is the best way to define and manage expectations, and provide the basis for measuring progress and contribution.

Many projects also lose and gain people during the execution of the project. When the project loses or gains members during its execution, it is important to develop the new team guidelines and meeting protocols. This is done for the same reason as in the beginning of the project - to facilitate relationships and prevent a conflict.

Lack of commitment, lack of interaction, and a lack of interest in constructively resolving conflict leads to an inability to work together towards a common goal.

The sponsor needs to be actively engaged with the team, be easily accessible and able to make things happen, so the team can move forward to its goals. There is something wrong with the sponsor or the senior management of the project if:

▸ team membership is layered on top of existing duties
▸ meetings are constantly delayed or cancelled because of other issues
▸ meetings with sponsors and leadership are difficult to schedule
▸ team questions do not get quick review and response

14

FBI virtual
case project

$170 million lost

management turnover, repeated requirements, changes, and violating Brooks' law

Virtual Case File (or VCF) was a software application developed by the United States Federal Bureau of Investigation between 2000 and 2005. The project was not close to completion when it was officially abandoned in January 2005, having turned into a complete fiasco for the FBI. In addition to wasting at least US $100 million, the failure brought widespread criticism to the bureau.

While the bureau claimed in testimony to Congress that the program lost $104 million in taxpayer money, some analysts believe the true figure is at least twice as high. In addition, the bureau continues to use the antiquated and inefficient ACS system, which could be hampering the bureau's new counter-terrorism mission.

In September 2000, the FBI announced the "Trilogy" program, intended to modernize the bureau's outdated IT infrastructure. The project was originally scheduled to take three years and cost $380 million and had three goals; purchasing modern desktop computers for all FBI offices, developing secure high-performance WAN and LAN networks, and modernizing the FBI's suite of investigative software applications.

The first two goals of Trilogy were generally successful, despite cost overruns. Replacing the Bureau's Automated Case Support (ACS) software system proved difficult. It had been developed in-house by the Bureau and was used to manage all documents relating to cases being investigated by the FBI, enabling agents to search and analyze evidence between different cases.

The software was originally intended to be deployed in mid-2004, and was originally intended to be little more than a web front-end to the existing ACS data. In December 2001 (after the September 11, 2001 attacks), the scope of VCF was changed with the goal being the complete replacement of all previous applications and migration of the existing data into an Oracle database. Additionally, the project's deadline was pushed up to December 2003. During project execution there were at least five different people in charge.

Initial development was based on meetings with users of the current ACS system. The resulting 800-page specification document was of poor quality. The contractor on the project, SAIC broke its programmers up into eight separate and sometimes competing teams, which struggled to communicate.

They chose to re-employ basic technologies like messaging, workflow, and e-mail rather than use existing software. Many developers complained about the lack of an overall plan for the project, and the project's schedule slipped throughout 2002.

One of the SAIC security engineers, Matthew Patton, tried to warn the government about the project failing, in response to a Senator's public statements a few days earlier about the importance of doing such projects well. This was regarded by FBI and SAIC management as attempting to "blow the whistle" on what he saw as crippling mismanagement of a national security-critical project. Patton was quickly removed from the project and eventually left SAIC for personal reasons.

In December 2002, the Bureau asked the United States Congress for increased funding, seeing it was well behind schedule. Congress approved an additional $123 million for the Trilogy project. In 2003, the project saw a quick succession of three different CIO's come and go. Despite development snags throughout 2003, SAIC delivered a version of VCF in December 2003.

The software was quickly deemed inadequate by the Bureau, who lamented multiple inadequacies in the software. SAIC claimed most of the FBI's complaints stemmed from specification changes they insisted upon after the fact. After months of argument, an independent arbitrator determined that both the FBI and SAIC were at fault.

On March 24, 2004, Director of the FBI Robert Mueller testified to Congress that the system would be operational by the summer, but most of the project's managers knew this would not happen.

SAIC claimed it would require over $50 million to get the system operational, which the Bureau refused to pay. Finally, in May 2004 the Bureau agreed to pay SAIC $16 million extra to attempt to salvage the system and also brought in Aerospace Corporation to review the project at a further cost of $2 million. Meanwhile, the Bureau had already begun talks for a replacement project beginning as early as 2005. Aerospace Corp.'s damning report was released in the Fall of 2004, at which point most observers knew the project was doomed. Development continued throughout 2004 until the project was officially scrapped in January 2005.

The project demonstrated a systematic failure of project management and software engineering practices, including:

▸ lack of a strong blueprint from the outset, leading to poor architectural decisions

▸ repeated changes in specification

▸ repeated management turnover, which contributed to the specification problem

▸ micromanagement of software developers

- the inclusion of many FBI personnel who had little or no formal training in computer science as managers and even engineers on the project

- scope creep as requirements were continually added to the system even as it was falling behind schedule

- code bloat due to changing specifications and scope creep, at one point it was estimated the software had over 700,000 lines of code

- violating Brooks' law by adding people and resources to the project as it was falling behind, slowing it further

- planned use of a flash cutover deployment, which made it difficult to adopt the system until it was perfected

15

The main reason projects fail

Projects rarely fail without prior warning signs. A warning sign is defined as an event or indication that predicts, cautions, or alerts one of possible or impending problems. There is hardly a project that seems to be doing great for six months or so before a sudden and unpredictable downfall.

Why do people ignore the signs of failure until the project is a complete disaster? Why are people so ignorant to not learn from the mistakes made by others? What do they do when evidence of failure conflicts with their beliefs that a project will be successful?

> "Red sky at night, sailors delight; red sky at morning, sailors warning"
>
> — Proverb

During the 1950s, behavioral psychologist Leon Festinger at Stanford University explained that people tend to ignore the evidence that conflicts with their beliefs until it becomes overwhelming. Festinger's theory (he called it the theory of cognitive dissonance) explains why the organization most commonly realizes that a project is failing at the end of the development schedule.

According to Festinger, if someone strongly supported the project at the start, this person will be inclined to ignore the negative signs while amplifying any positive scraps that can be found, until the project collapses in total failure.

Advanced Project solutions research: failed projects identification

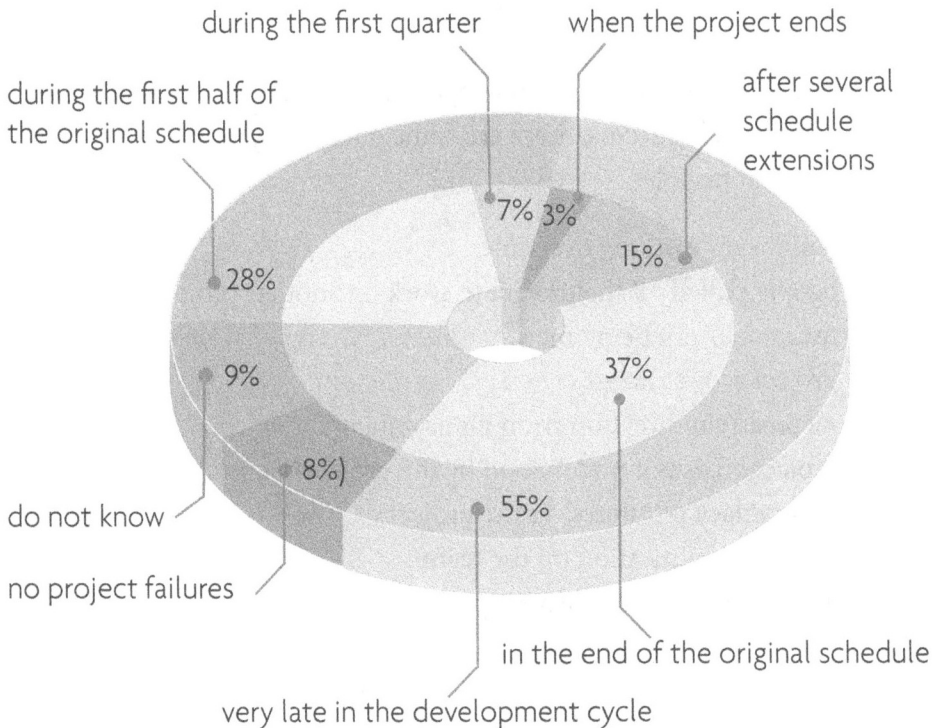

Ignoring signs of failure

Every failed project had more than one reason to fail. It's not just that this project failed purely because of communication problems and that one because of improper stakeholder management. Many analyzed failed projects provide evidence that they failed because of multiple reasons.

After the project fails the team members usually recall many warning signs which were ignored or not properly evaluated. This means that it's impossible to miss all warning signs as there are always many of them.

> Often the only difference between a project's complete failure and its success is in spotting warning signs.

Besides the standard project management metrics, which are used to measure project success, these are some obvious signs which mean the project is in trouble:

- employees working overtime
- people pulled off the project to work on another project
- milestones not being met
- project scope changes
- inconsistent direction from management
- project goals not understood by the project team
- general lack of interest in the project
- poor communication on the team
- fear of talking about project problems

16

How to prevent project failure

It is necessary to take a proactive approach to prevent a project failure. Any red flags should be evaluated if they are serious enough to warrant project termination or significant redirection. Using an early warning system, organizations can save considerable resources simply by identifying failed projects while they are still in the early stages.

> "One timely cry of warning can save nine of surprise."
>
> — Joshua Thompson

The research entitled "Silence Fails: The Five Crucial Conversations for Flawless Execution" carried out by training company VitalSmarts and professional services firm, The Concours Group, has uncovered five crucial issues that have an enormous impact on whether high-stakes business initiatives succeed or fail. The main reason for project failures is the inability of team members, the project manager and the sponsor to hold accountability or admit and openly discuss any problems with a project.

The report found that fewer than one in five project leaders effectively engage in the crucial conversations needed to solve problems. The study also found that it's not enough just to speak up, it should be done efficiently. Some managers speak up but water down their concerns, so the issues are never fully aired. Some speak up but do so in a way that provokes defensiveness from others. Only a handful - about one in eight - is able to share their full concerns and feel their views are understood.

> The lesson to be drawn from this is simple: "Unless and until leaders take measures to ensure their environment is conducive to holding crucial conversations, a significant number of these issues will remain unaddressed, invisible, and fatal".

If there is just one behavior to be rewarded, it is to praise those who are breaking the vicious circle of silence. The report concludes: "If you want to change the values of an organization away from silence and toward candid dialogue, make heroes of those who take a chance with these new behaviors".

If you get a bad feeling about a project, you need to try to work out the cause of the discomfort and identify the source of the issue. As many failed projects have shown, it is tempting to ignore your instincts and hope that things will go the way you would like. But if you're feeling it, you're feeling it for a reason. Do not ever ignore it! You can fix some things by explaining your concerns and discussing.

Bibliography

Concours Group. (2005). Silence Fails: The Five Crucial Conversations for Flawless Execution. *http://www.silencefails.com/*

Cushing, K. (2002). Why Projects Fail. Computer Weekly, November 21, 2005, 58.

Dudley, C., Gelman, L., Peterson, W.J. (2001). ERP Trends. The Conference Board. *http://www.conference-board.org/publications/ publicationdetail.cfm?publicationid=465*

Festinger, L. (1957). A theory of cognitive dissonance. Stanford, CA: Stanford University Press.

Flyvbjerg, B., Holm, M.S., and Buhlthat, S. (2002). Underestimating costs in public works projects.Journal of the American Planning Assosication, Vol. 68, No. 3. Chicago, IL. *http://flyvbjerg.plan.aau.dk/JAPAASPUBLISHED.pdf*

Fraser, S. (2002). Costs of Implementing the Canadian Firearms Program.Auditor General of Canada. Chapter 10 Department of Justice. *http://www.oag-bvg.gc.ca/domino/reports.nsf/html/02menu_e.html*

Gartner Group. (1996). Project Management Skills: Avoiding Management by Crisis.

IT Cortex. (2004). Project failure statistics. *http://www.it-cortex.com/Stat_Failure_Cause.htm* (Bull Survey)

IT Cortex. (2004). Statistics over IT projects failure rate.
http://www.it-cortex.com/Stat_Failure_Rate.htm
(Robbins-Gioia, KPMG, OASIG)

McCarter, J. (2009). Ontario's Electronic Health Records Initiative.
Auditor General of Ontario. Special Report.
http://69.164.72.173/en/reports_en/ehealth_en.pdf

Standish Group. (1995). Chaos Report, 1995.
http://www.projectsmart.co.uk/docs/chaos-report.pdf

Standish Group. (2004). Chaos Report, 2004.
http://www.standishgroup.com/custom_chronicles/classic.php

Vespa, R. (2008). âTwo reasons Why IT Projects Continue To Fail.CIO.
http://advice.cio.com/remi/two_reasons_why_it_projects_continue_to_fail
(Dynamic Markets Report)

Photo credits

Cover
psdGraphics

p. 6
http://journeytopeak.com

p. 16
http://slapfish.com

p. 19
Sydney Opera House: *http://wallpaper.sk*
Concorde supersonic airplane: *http://www.*
freecomputerdesktopwallpaper.com/

p. 20
Boston's Big Dig: *http:// constructionequipmentguide.com*
Channel tunnel: *photo by Scott Barbour/Getty Images)*

p. 22
http://bpelite.com/

p. 23
http://www.flickr.com/photos/wili/206909928/

p. 26
http://www.flickr.com/photos/wheatfields/2587147000/

p. 30
http://www.flickr.com/photos/joshfassbind/4584323789/

p. 37
http://www.solarviews.com/

p. 40
http://fadyart.com/

p. 46
Getty Images

p. 53
Washington Times

p. 56
http://www.l2lgroup.com/

p. 67
CTV

p. 72
http://www.flickr.com/photos/8078381@N03/2614922363/

p. 83
The Globe and Mail

p. 88
Photobucket

p. 104
http://blog.cleanenergy.org/

p. 108
iStockphoto

www.ingramcontent.com/pod-product-compliance
Lightning Source LLC
Chambersburg PA
CBHW051414200326
41520CB00023B/7236